A POCKET GUIDE TO
THE HOLY ROSARY

KEVIN AND MARY O'NEILL
BUILDING BLOCKS OF FAITH SERIES

SOPHIA INSTITUTE PRESS
Manchester, New Hampshire

This revised and expanded 2022 edition of the Building Blocks of Faith series *A Pocket Guide to the Holy Rosary* is based on the 2021 Storytel Press publication of the same title. Text and images have been adapted from the Building Blocks of Faith series' *Catechism of the Seven Sacraments*.

Copyright © 2021, 2022 by Kevin and Mary O'Neill
Cover by Perceptions Studios
Printed in the United States of America. All rights reserved.

Scripture texts in this work are taken from the New American Bible, revised edition © 2010, 1991, 1986, 1970 Confraternity of Christian Doctrine, Washington, D.C. and are used by permission of the copyright owner. All Rights Reserved. No part of the New American Bible may be reproduced in any form without permission in writing from the copyright owner.

Excerpts from the English translation of the Catechism of the Catholic Church for use in the United States of America copyright © 1994, United States Catholic Conference, Inc.—Libreria Editrice Vaticana. English translation of the Catechism of the Catholic Church: Modifications from the Editio Typica copyright © 1997, United States Conference of Catholic Bishops—Libreria Editrice Vaticana.

LEGO®, the brick configuration, and the minifigure are all trademarks of the LEGO Group, which does not sponsor, authorize, or endorse this book.

No part of this book may be reproduced, stored in a retrieval system, or transmitted in any form, or by any means, electronic, mechanical, photocopying, or otherwise, without the prior written permission of the publisher, except by a reviewer, who may quote brief passages in a review.

Sophia Institute Press
Box 5284, Manchester, NH 03108
1-800-888-9344
www.SophiaInstitute.com

Sophia Institute Press® is a registered trademark of Sophia Institute.

print ISBN: 978-1-64413-878-6
ebook ISBN: 978-1-64413-879-3

Library of Congress Control Number: 2022948564

A POCKET GUIDE TO
THE HOLY ROSARY

THE JOYFUL MYSTERIES

(Monday and Saturday; and the Sundays from the 1st Sunday of Advent until Lent.)

1. The Annunciation to Mary
2. The Visitation of Mary
3. The Birth of Our Lord Jesus Christ
4. The Presentation of the Child Jesus in the Temple
5. The Finding of Our Lord in the Temple

THE SORROWFUL MYSTERIES

(Tuesday and Friday; and the Sundays of Lent.)

1. The Agony of Christ in the Garden
2. The Scourging at the Pillar
3. The Crowning with Thorns
4. The Carrying of the Cross
5. The Crucifixion and Death of Our Lord on the Cross

THE GLORIOUS MYSTERIES

(Wednesday; and the Sundays from Easter until Advent.)

1. The Resurrection of Our Lord
2. The Ascension of Our Lord
3. The Descent of the Holy Spirit upon the Apostles
4. The Assumption of the Blessed Virgin Mary into Heaven
5. The Coronation of Our Lady as Queen of Heaven and Earth

THE LUMINIOUS MYSTERIES

(Thursdays.)

1. Jesus' Baptism in the Jordan
2. The Wedding at Cana
3. The Proclamation of the Kingdom
4. The Transfiguration
5. The Institution of the Eucharist

THE ROSARY HAS FIVE DECADES, AND WE MEDITATE ON A DIFFERENT MYSTERY OF CHRIST'S LIFE FOR EACH DECADE. WHILE PRAYING A ROSARY, WE CHOOSE ONE OF FOUR SETS OF MYSTERIES TO FOCUS ON: THE JOYFUL, SORROWFUL, LUMINOUS, OR GLORIOUS MYSTERIES.

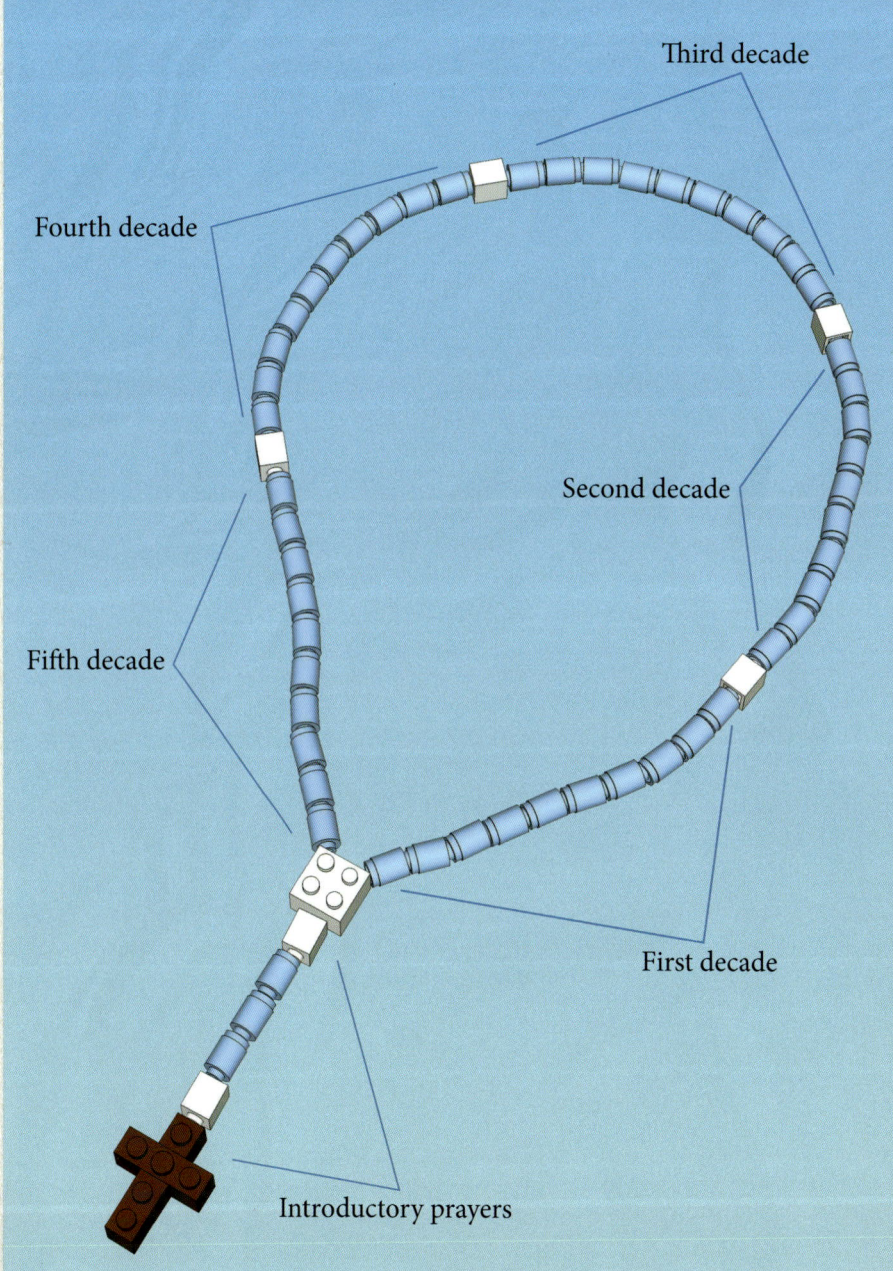

Third decade

Fourth decade

Second decade

Fifth decade

First decade

Introductory prayers

The Holy Rosary

THE **JOYFUL MYSTERIES** CONTEMPLATE THE JOYFUL TIMES IN JESUS' LIFE.

READ ABOUT THE MYSTERIES IN YOUR BIBLE

MONDAY AND SATURDAY

THE FIRST JOYFUL MYSTERY IS THE ANNUNCIATION.

LUKE 1:26-38

THE SECOND JOYFUL MYSTERY IS THE VISITATION.

LUKE 1:39-40

THE THIRD JOYFUL MYSTERY IS THE NATIVITY.

THE FOURTH JOYFUL MYSTERY IS THE PRESENTATION.

THE FIFTH JOYFUL MYSTERY IS THE FINDING OF JESUS IN THE TEMPLE.

THE **SORROWFUL MYSTERIES** CONTEMPLATE THE SAD TIMES IN JESUS' LIFE.

THE FIRST SORROWFUL MYSTERY IS THE AGONY IN THE GARDEN.

THE SECOND SORROWFUL MYSTERY IS THE SCOURGING AT THE PILLAR.

THE **GLORIOUS MYSTERIES** CONTEMPLATE THE PLAN OF SALVATION.

WEDNESDAY AND SUNDAY

THE FIRST GLORIOUS MYSTERY IS THE RESURRECTION.

THE SECOND GLORIOUS MYSTERY IS THE ASCENSION.

12

THE THIRD GLORIOUS MYSTERY IS THE DESCENT OF THE HOLY SPIRIT.

THE FIFTH GLORIOUS MYSTERY IS THE CORONATION.

THE FOURTH GLORIOUS MYSTERY IS THE ASSUMPTION.

REV. 12:1

HERE'S HOW TO PRAY THE ROSARY.

1 **Sign of the Cross:** In the name of the Father, and of the Son, and of the Holy Spirit. Amen.

Apostles' Creed: I believe in God, the Father Almighty, Creator of Heaven and earth. I believe in Jesus Christ, His only Son, our Lord. He was conceived by the power of the Holy Spirit and born of the Virgin Mary. He suffered under Pontius Pilate, was crucified, died, and was buried. He descended into hell. On the third day He rose again. He ascended into Heaven and is seated at the right hand of the Father. He will come again to judge the living and the dead. I believe in the Holy Spirit, the holy Catholic Church, the communion of saints, the forgiveness of sins, the resurrection of the body, and the life everlasting. Amen.

2 **Our Father** who art in Heaven, hallowed be Thy Name; Thy Kingdom come; Thy will be done on earth as it is in Heaven. Give us this day our daily bread, and forgive us our trespasses, as we forgive those who trespass against us, and lead us not into temptation, but deliver us from evil. Amen.

3 **Hail Mary**, full of grace, the Lord is with thee. Blessed art thou amongst women, and blessed is the fruit of thy womb, Jesus. Holy Mary, Mother of God, pray for us sinners, now and at the hour of our death. Amen.

4 **Glory be** to the Father, and to the Son, and to the Holy Spirit, as it was in the beginning, is now, and ever shall be, world without end. Amen.

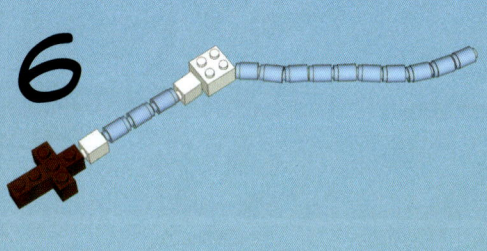

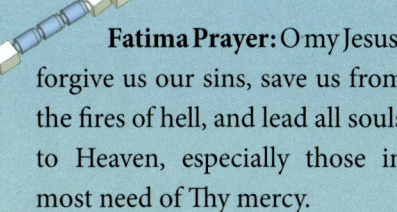

Fatima Prayer: O my Jesus, forgive us our sins, save us from the fires of hell, and lead all souls to Heaven, especially those in most need of Thy mercy.

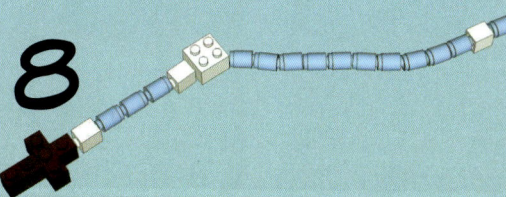

ROSARY INSTRUCTIONS

Start by choosing which set of mysteries you will meditate on. Suggestions: Joyful on Monday & Saturday, Luminous on Thursday, Sorrowful on Tuesday & Friday, Glorious on Wednesday & Sunday.

1. Begin with the Sign of the Cross, followed by the Apostles' Creed prayer.

2. Pray one Our Father prayer, also called The Lord's Prayer.

3. Pray three Hail Mary prayers for the virtues of faith, hope, and charity.

4. Pray one Glory Be prayer.

5. State the first mystery, and pray one Our Father prayer.

6. Pray 10 Hail Mary prayers while contemplating the stated mystery.

7. Conclude the decade by praying the Glory Be prayer and the Fatima Prayer.

8. Continue saying four more decades, meditating on each of the five mysteries in order.

9. Conclude the decades by praying the Hail Holy Queen prayer.

10. Some people also recite the Rosary Prayer, the *Memorare*, and the Prayer to St. Michael the Archangel. Some also recite one Our Father prayer, one Hail Mary prayer, and one Glory Be prayer for the intentions of the pope.

11. Finally, conclude with the Sign of the Cross.

9 **Hail, Holy Queen**, mother of mercy, our life, our sweetness, and our hope. To thee do we cry, poor banished children of Eve. To thee do we send up our sighs, mourning and weeping in this valley of tears. Turn then, most gracious advocate, thine eyes of mercy toward us, and after this our exile show us the blessed fruit of thy womb, Jesus. O clement, O loving, O sweet Virgin Mary. Pray for us, O Holy Mother of God. That we may be made worthy of the promises of Christ.

> OKAY, CYNTHIA, LET'S OFFER THIS ROSARY FOR THE HOLY FATHER AND FOR HEALTH IN OUR FAMILIES.

The Rosary Prayer: Let us pray: O God, whose Only Begotten Son, by His life, death, and resurrection, has purchased for us the rewards of eternal life, grant, we beseech Thee, that while meditating on these mysteries of the most holy Rosary of the Blessed Virgin Mary, we may imitate what they contain and obtain what they promise, through the same Christ our Lord. Amen.

Memorare: Remember, O most gracious Virgin Mary, that never was it known that anyone who fled to thy protection, implored thy help, or sought thine intercession was left unaided. Inspired by this confidence, I fly unto thee, O Virgin of virgins, my mother; to thee do I come, before thee I stand, sinful and sorrowful. O Mother of the Word incarnate, despise not my petitions, but in thy mercy hear and answer me. Amen. For the Pope's intentions: **Our Father …**, **Hail Mary …**, **Glory Be …**, **Prayer to St. Michael the Archangel:** St. Michael the Archangel, defend us in battle. Be our protection against the wickedness and snares of the devil. May God rebuke him, we humbly pray, and do thou, O Prince of the heavenly host, by the power of God, cast into hell Satan, and all the evil spirits, who prowl about the world seeking the ruin of souls. Amen.

Sign of the Cross: In the name of the Father, and of the Son, and of the Holy Spirit. Amen.

EXPLORE THE ENTIRE
BUILDING BLOCKS OF FAITH SERIES

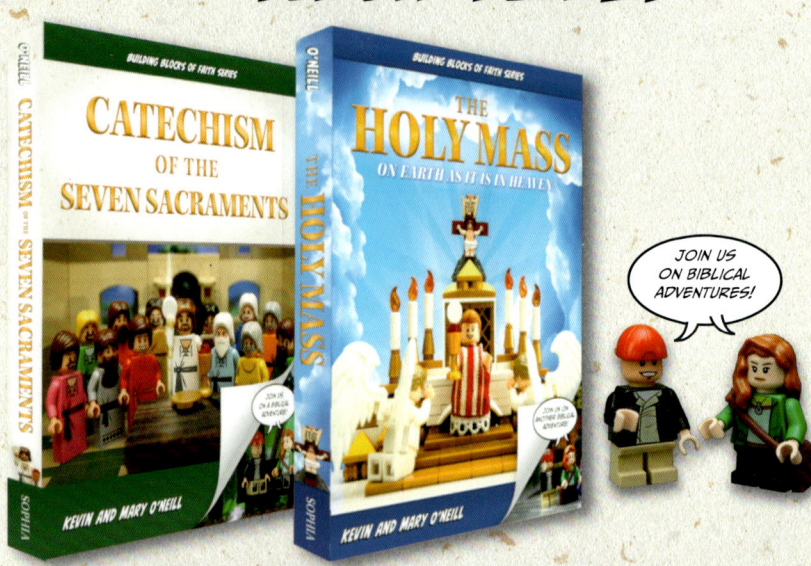

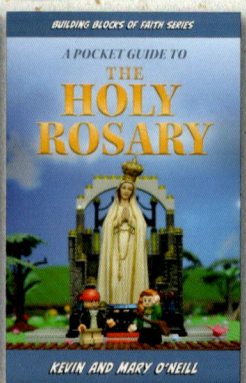

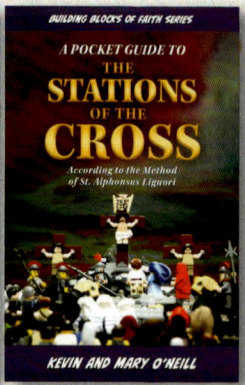

The ***Building Blocks of Faith*** series works to create and share solidly orthodox materials to help families build their own domestic churches, and, in turn, to build and strengthen the Body of Christ. Our books use typology to explain the foundations of the Faith. We illustrate our graphic novels by building, designing, and photographing intricate sets — built with your child's favorite building-block toys! We strive to spread the Gospel, help the Faith come alive, create disciples, and promote the call to evangelization, as we do our part to build God's Kingdom.

www.sophiainstitute.com/BuildingBlocks